ONCE MORE, WITH FEELING

REVISING YOUR MANUSCRIPT

JODY LYNN NYE

ONCE MORE, WITH FEELING
Copyright © 2019 Jody Lynn Nye

All rights reserved. No part of this book may be reproduced or transmitted in any form or by any electronic or mechanical means, including photocopying, recording or by any information storage and retrieval system, without the express written permission of the copyright holder, except where permitted by law.

The authors and publisher have strived to be as accurate and complete as possible in creating the Million Dollar Writing series. We don't believe in magical outcomes from our advice. We do believe in hard work and helping others. The advice in our Million Dollar Writing series is intended to offer new tools and approaches to writing. We make no guarantees about any individual's ability to get results or earn money with our ideas, information, tools or strategies. We do want to help by giving great content, direction and strategies to move writers forward faster. Nothing in this book is a promise or guarantee of future book sales or earnings. Any numbers referenced in this series are estimates or projections, and should not be considered exact, actual or as a promise of potential earnings. All numbers are for the purpose of illustration. The sole purpose of these materials is to educate and entertain. Any perceived slights to specific organizations or individuals are unintentional. The publisher and authors are not engaged in rendering legal, accounting, financial, or other professional services. If legal or expert assistance is required, the services of a competent professional should be sought.

EBook ISBN: 978-1-68057-064-9
Trade Paperback ISBN: 978-1-68057-065-6
Cover design by **Janet McDonald**
Cover artwork images by **Adobe Stock**
Art Director Kevin J. Anderson
Published by
WordFire Press LLC
PO Box 1840
Monument CO 80132

Kevin J. Anderson & Rebecca Moesta, Publishers

WordFire Press eBook Edition 2019
WordFire Press Trade Paperback Edition 2019

Printed in the USA

Join our WordFire Press Readers Group for
sneak previews, updates, new projects, and giveaways.
Sign up at wordfirepress.com

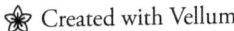 Created with Vellum

DEDICATION

To Bill, my first and best beta reader

FOREWORD

Congratulations! You finished a book. You're exhausted and excited. When you typed the words "The End" (or just acknowledged that the final period was the last one), you ascended into an echelon that fewer than two percent of all the would-be writers ever do: the ones who have finished something that they wrote.

Go ahead and pat yourself on the back. It's a real attainment. You have every reason to be proud. You put your ideas on paper (let's be real: on your hard drive). If it was nonfiction, you organized your facts and checked them, presented them in an interesting manner, and concluded with your observations about your chosen subject. If it was fiction, you built a world from scratch, peopled it with characters whom you like and believe in, set them on a journey in which they succeeded or failed to accomplish their goal, and had fun doing it.

You had fun, didn't you? If you didn't, I promise

you your readers will be able to tell. But we can handle that part later.

Now is the time to celebrate in the way that you like best. Pop the champagne cork, buy yourself something to commemorate, go out to dinner with loved ones, sleep without feeling that the book is going to kick you out of bed in the middle of the night to write something you forgot. Take a break.

(Musical interlude)

Did you take a break? Good.

Now it's time to move onto the next stage. No, it isn't where you attach the document to a message and send it to your agent or publisher or an online book publication service. It's time to revise your manuscript.

When you write, you write as a reader. You wrote this book because you believed that it didn't exist before, and it needed to. You put into the story everything that you would love to find in a book. You fulfilled those fantasies. Scratched those itches. Brought the story to a satisfying and appropriate conclusion. Well done. Really. There is no sarcasm here. I mean it.

When you revise, though, you need to read it as an editor. Now is the time to make the book the best you can make it. Let's begin.

WHY REVISE?

The book you just finished is not the one you began. Just as in war where no plan survives contact with the enemy, no story comes out precisely as you conceived and planned it. Your subconscious mind took hold of the outline or notes with which you started and smoothed out the inconsistencies or implausible elements as you continued to write. It might have steered away from the original plot. Most of the time those changes are for the better, because you will have learned more about the story, the characters, and the setting as you went along, and your subconscious incorporated all that information into the manuscript. Once you were writing, any awkwardness you might have had at first settled into the style that the book now incorporates.

This book is not Writing 101. If by now you don't know how to construct a narrative or use dialogue, you're reading a manual on how to revise your book too soon. Many books in the *Million Dollar Writing* line (WordFire Press) will help you to write your book. Revision is needed once you have actually finished a manuscript. You can get the basics on plotting and story construction from those or numerous other sources, such as the *Save the Cat!* series by Blake Snyder, *The Anatomy of Story* by John Truby, Stephen King's *On Writing*, Neil Gaiman's master class, former SFWA president Cat Rambo's brilliant online tutorials, Dwight V. Swain's *Techniques of the Selling Writer*, and the long-running *Writing Excuses* podcast. Come on back when you're finished and ready to revise.

Robert A. Heinlein, known as the "dean of science fiction writers" offered five rules of writing:

1. You must write.
2. You must finish what you write.
3. You must refrain from rewriting, except to editorial order.
4. You must put the work on the market.
5. You must keep the work on the market until it is sold.

Hence, you have entered stage three, but instead of waiting for an editor to tell you what s/he wants, you are going to go over it and improve it yourself.

As a rule, most writers finish a piece before going back to revise. One of the chief reasons for that is going back over finished material and fiddling with it may distract them from going forward to finish it. Another is that as you write the rest of the book you may find that you need to change things in earlier chapters, nullifying some of your revision. Mario Puzo, author of *The Godfather*, had ten rules for writing. One of them was never to show anything unfinished to anyone, because it might cause you to doubt your piece. Have confidence in yourself, but confidence does not mean you are infallible, so it's good advice to finish it anyhow. Thousands of distractions abound in the world. Your mind will retain more of the small details if you don't allow a prolonged interval between beginning and finishing. If you had to put the book down for a while, it's all the more important to go over it in detail now, to make certain your plot went where you intended it to, added all the small touches you wanted, and incorporate other interesting ideas that you have thought of since you last worked on it.

On the other hand, Dean Wesley Smith, author of over one hundred novels and editor of Fiction River Press edits as he goes, as does Timothy Zahn, bestselling author of the Star Wars: Thrawn series, and the late Gene Wolfe, author of the Book of the New Sun novels. It's also my writing style. From long experience, we can go back without losing the energy of what we are doing. We don't recommend this method for beginners, because it will interfere with the flow of creation and getting things down on paper while they are still fresh.

More common is the method used by bestselling author and publisher of WordFire Press Kevin J. Anderson, who will do up to seven revisions after he has finished his first draft. He continues to tweak and improve the piece over time, giving it that polish that his readers have come to expect.

Above all, we want you to *finish what you write*, as in Heinlein's Rule Two above.

Don't overwork your story so much that it gets stale. You have to learn when to let it go. Yes, there will always be errors of which you are aware. Almost no one else will ever see them. And, yes, as you are walking back from the mailbox looking at your first copy (as I did), and you will open it to the page with the one and only typo on it. Relax. All you need to do is make your book the best you can *now* while retaining the enthusiasm you put into it while writing it.

If you have the time, put your finished work aside until you've forgotten *how* you wrote it. That could take a couple of weeks to years. Most people don't have that leisure, so you will have to set your writing mind aside and assume your editorial side. Bestselling writer and teacher Michael A. Stackpole says, "When you edit, you are in a different place than when you write." You do have an editorial side—you used it while writing when you made grammatical and word choices. Now you're going to put it to work full-time.

First of all, set aside all distractions and read the manuscript through. Try not to see things that are not there. Pretend it's someone else's book. You must read *only* the words on the page. Jot down notes as you go. You want to record your first impressions as the editor. These are the things you will correct on the next pass.

You can use Track Changes or other marking software to indicate places in the manuscript that will receive further scrutiny later. If you prefer to work on hard copy, print it out and use a pen of any color than black so your edits will be more visible.

An important reason to read your manuscript straight through now is to spot repetition. When you look at it with fresh eyes, you will see where you might have repeated a phrase, a description, or even a whole scene that you had written then rewritten, but not deleted one version or the other. Make a note to go back to those. Your helpful subconscious will begin to make decisions about them, which you can incorporate later.

IN THE BEGINNING

Does your story start off with a figurative bang? Are you drawn into the story from the first few sentences? If not, what are you missing? Do you know where you are? Whose story is this? What do you need to know about this world from the very start that will lead you into the extended story?

NARRATIVE HOOK

All editors look for a narrative hook. That is a literary technique in the opening of any story that "hooks" the reader's attention so that he or she will keep on reading. It's the first impression that will set the story in time and place, establish at least one character (though not necessarily the main character), will include an action of some kind, and will provoke a question in the mind of the reader that can only be answered by going on to read the rest of the book. Some authors readers can do it in a sentence or two, figuratively smacking the reader upside the head and intriguing them. John Scalzi did this brilliantly in his award-winning book, *Old Man's War*. Others will use the entire first chapter, laying important background as they go, as Robin Hobb did in *Assassin's Apprentice*.

For examples, go to your own library and read the first sentence, paragraph or pages of your favorite titles. Ask yourself what they have that made you keep reading. You must have a hook. Do you?

With those elements in mind, write your hook as economically as you can. In a short story, you don't have that much real estate to build on. Try to use no more than a few paragraphs. In a novel, do your best to keep it under ten pages, and those pages must be as tight as you can make them. This is the point at which you would lose a casual reader. Don't let that happen.

The hook is no place for extraneous exposition. While it might be fun to *you* to show the reader what it's like to zoom in on your planet all the way from the heliopause, it's even more fun for the *reader* if you show it from the point of view of an interesting character, and explain why the character is zooming in toward that planet, and what is at stake when s/he reaches it. Save the cinematic and graphic description for the movie script. Stories are about people. If you had not introduced one, anyone, now is the time.

Narrative hooks are a terrific way for a writer to

learn to create a compelling scene that is concise and interesting. When you finish editing this story, try a few just for fun. You can keep them as writing prompts for later.

WHO IS IN THIS STORY?

So often in the beginning of a book by a new writer, the reader is given no character to follow, only a nebulously presented world. Other new writers will think this is the time to be mysterious and interesting, keeping facts from the reader, but it can backfire spectacularly. The famous unnamed character is a pain in the butt. "He walked into the saloon, gun belt slung low on his hips." *Name* her, him, xe, it, or them. Names can suggest much about the type of story to come, whether it's Regency romance, science fiction, high fantasy, or mainstream fiction. Do you have Zog, Lady Patricia Herschweimer, Engineer Apprentice Kron'ac, or Tracy Chang? That's not to say you shouldn't play against type in your book—make your storytelling unique and memorable—but name your character. They'll learn it soon enough, or they should. Do it now. Yes, there are exceptions, such as in Ralph Ellison's groundbreaking novel *Invisible Man*, whose first-person narrator never has a name, but his anonymity is the heartbreaking point of his story. It's doubtful that that is true of yours. Name your characters for the reader as soon as you can.

That said, a hook doesn't always feature the protagonist. Anyone will do who can set the scene for your narrative. Consider the opening, or teaser, of every *Law and Order* episode ever aired. Two people are walking down the street. One of them trips over something, and looks down in shock to see that it's the outstretched arm of a corpse. Dun dun!

FIND A WAY TO DESCRIBE YOUR CHARACTER, EVEN A LITTLE

Their personal characteristics are more interesting than mere details of height, weight, eye color, and so on. "Myron's arthritis made his knees ache as he hurried to open the door." That's enough. It tells you something about the character, and implies more. Your reader will create a mental picture useful for this scene. Make sure that the facets you reveal now are important to the moment. Save the rest for after the hook has been achieved. Now, where is this character?

SET THE SCENE

Did you deposit your reader into a blank setting with only voices to keep them company? On every page, ask yourself if the people and things important to the story or scene are described. Can your reader visualize them from what you have written? Description is the bugbear of the new writer. The reader needs a basis for understanding your story, and the location makes a huge impact. Lack of description that gives your reader a picture of your universe is a rookie mistake. It may be clear as a photograph in your mind, but the reader cannot see what you imagine. Your job is to create your world with words that will be memorable enough to leave a lasting image in their memory so that the reader does not need to refer back to a previous page. This does not mean turgid prose, but rather clear description often using more than one of the senses.

Give a vivid image instead, one that will stick in the reader's mind even when they put the book down. "The entry hall to the great library with its walls inlaid with fourteen colors of marble always awed Hitomi." Don't overburden your reader with every small detail of your world—not yet—but give them enough to know where they are and what is important. Here is where you can point to details that they will want to remember later, but those must fit seamlessly into the hook.

WHAT'S HAPPENING?

What is worth your reader's while to keep reading? Did you detail every step the character took since he woke up?[1] That will bog down your narrative. Keep the action moving. Begin with something that happens or has just happened.

All stories really begin when something changes. What has changed in this person's world? Why are you starting your story here and now? You are pointing to an important *initiating event*. If that isn't here, you may be beginning too early.

The last part of the narrative hook is the hook itself.

What makes the reader's mouth drop open? What makes it irresistible to go on and turn the page? Stating simple facts aren't enough. How did the preceding event come about? You know it. Tantalize your reader with a hint.

"A massive, green-scaled body crashed through the ceiling of the condo and landed at Denise's feet, spraying shards of drywall and insulation all over the room. The lanky teenager looked from the panting dragon to the ancient leather-bound book in her hand, up at the ceiling, and back again. The summoning spell had worked! But what was she going to tell Aunt Nadine? She wouldn't buy the same excuse as last time."

The hook at the end, *last time*, tells you that there is a back story, at least one previous instance, and that Denise had managed to get out of trouble then. Scene set, character introduced, description included, complications presented, and questions established.

WHERE DO YOU SEE YOUR HOOK?

Take a look at your opening paragraphs. If a hook does not stand out, ask yourself what's important about this opening scene that compels the reader to want to know more. Is it many pages later? Ask yourself if you are building toward a necessary conclusion with attendant rising tension, or if you've larded up your opening with back story or exposition that could come later, incorporated seamlessly into future scenes, or be deleted altogether. Your hook should, simply, hook the reader.

---

1. By the way, editors hate stories that begin with the main character waking up. They get so many submissions like that, and it's justified in very few cases. Find another way to initiate your narrative.

READ ON AS IF YOU HAVE NEVER SEEN THIS BOOK BEFORE

SPEED BUMPS

If you find you enjoy what you're reading and read only the words that are there not what you intended to say, good for you, but it means you're going to have to concentrate so you don't miss potential flaws that do need editing. If you manage to read all the way through without stopping and still enjoy it as if it was someone else's book, that's good news. Your manuscript may need only a little polish before you can begin to submit it.

If instead you find yourself distracted even a little while trying to read your story, that's a red flag. What's wrong here? Have you left too many unanswered questions to burden the reader? The more questions and images you leave vague or uncertain, the more resentment builds up in the reader's mind. Answer everything as quickly as you can in context. Only questions fundamental to your plot should remain unanswered.

What might be some of those unnecessary mysteries? What are you trying to keep as a surprise? So often, none of what you do not want to reveal *now* is vital to the structure of the narrative. Is our heroine the daughter of the king? That will color every interaction she has. Reveal it. Is she secretly affianced? You may hold that one. Is she gay? That ought to be foreshadowed if not revealed, depending on the needs of the story. Does she have a "true name" no one else must know? That you can keep secret, as long as you have something to call her in the meanwhile. If she's a secret agent, you can surprise the reader with that fact later, as long as they can follow what else is going on, and have hints that she is not entirely what she seems.

This has nothing to do with keeping secrets from the characters. It's *their* journey to enlightenment that we're following. Baffle them as you need to.

PURPOSE

Does every scene need to be there? Your job as the storyteller is to get in, do what needs to be done, then get out. Each and every scene must move the plot, tell the reader something she will need to know now or later, or tell something about the character. If it doesn't do at least one, and preferably all three, consider what made you want to include it in the first place. As the editor, your job is to make sure you did this, and be merciless about what is not needed.

If you can't justify that a scene is needed or adds to

the tale, boot it. You may be in love with what you wrote and it may be really outstanding prose, but no matter how well written or beautifully worded the part is, if it does not contribute it should not be there. There is not a place for the most elegant painting in the middle of a street. Being ruthless with your irrelevant text does not mean losing those words forever. Save the scene for another story where it will fit, and file off the serial numbers. No writing is wasted, only out of place.

POINT OF VIEW

Who is "telling" this story? Do you have a consistent point-of-view character throughout? Who is your protagonist? It is not necessarily the POV character. Dr. John Watson is our guide through the stories he is purported to have written, but Sherlock Holmes is the protagonist. The protagonist is the one who causes the climax of the story to come about and resolve the plot. The POV character is the one introducing the reader to your world, so what that person has a tendency to notice—and the capacity for noticing it—is what the reader knows.

Is the writer speaking directly to the reader, as Charlotte Bronte did in *Jane Eyre*? "Reader, I married him." Or, rather, does the POV character merely relate the tale in their own way? The distinction here makes the reader feel more or less involved. The choice of style is yours.

Be aware of breaking the fourth wall, that invisible barrier that separates the reader from the story. In most books, the characters are unaware that they are fictional beings in a story constructed by you, the author. Once in a while, often in farces, one or more point of view characters will interact with the real world. In *Bored of the Rings* by the Harvard Lampoon, one of the Boggies wonders how much longer their quest will take, and looks at the thick wad of pages still being held in the reader's right hand. Bear in mind that type of scene or dialogue can take the reader out of the story. Be prepared to reestablish that narrative context.

Are you using more than one POV character? Make certain that you check in with each from time to time. Don't let the reader wonder what has happened to the third character just because you don't have anything for her to do for sixteen chapters. If she's important enough to carry the plot along, her story line should experience rising tension and be heading for a satisfying conclusion just as the others do. If you find yourself wondering what happened to that character, it's certain that your readers will be wondering the same thing. Don't have your antagonist or villain finally appear so far into the book that the reader has stopped watching for one.

NARRATIVE VOICE

Just as important as the point-of-view character is the narrative voice. This is one of the most obvious changes that you will find by going back to read over your work. When you start to write, you're toying with style, seeing what will work best. Most of the time, you'll fall into one voice as you go, but if you interrupt the writing for any length of time, you may begin again with a slightly different approach. Go over it again and change it so you are consistent in the way you present your prose from beginning to end.

In most cases, the narration ought to be invisible, written in standard grammar, setting scenes, describing characters, and allowing the action to take place without interference. If you choose to have an opinionated narrative style, with comments upon the action *not from the point of view of any of the characters*, it can be very distracting, or effective, depending on how skilled you are at using it.

At the same time, you need also to decide if the book will be told in the first person, which automatically makes it an intimate treatment, or one of the third person styles.

First-person narration is common for young adult literature, although not ubiquitous. Your character is telling his own story. That means all of his personality traits come through, including his blind spots, prejudices, fears, and other human elements should be present throughout. This style is appealing because the reader sees everything that the character does, so the story unfolds as it happens to that character. First person has greater immediacy than third person, but it's also limited in scope to that character's experience and ability to understand the events in which he is embroiled.

An important type of first-person style is the "unreliable narrator." The actions in the novel are firmly in your character's point of view, but may not be accurate or true as far as what actually happens. Depending on the character's personality, he might be lying to himself, deluded, or firmly entrenched in a certain mindset that doesn't want to be persuaded (allowing for growth and change by the end of the story, by the way). If yours is an unreliable narrator, keep track of reality versus the character's view of it, so that when the actual chain of events impinges, the progression has a logical feel to it.

Third person intimate allows the reader to hear the thoughts and see the actions of one character at a time, but cannot know anything that the character herself does not know. Third person omniscient can see what is going on elsewhere, such as behind the character's back. This style is also useful for multiple points of view, as it will feel less jarring when moving to another character's mind.

Third person can have a great deal of personality based upon the traits of the POV character. William Faulkner, in his novel *The Sound and the Fury*, has several sections each from the perspective of a person with a specific narrative voice, even though those sections do not speak directly to the reader. One is a developmentally disabled man, who repeats himself frequently, and has a childlike vocabulary compared with other narrators. Another is a young woman whose observations are kindly but self-centered.

Dorothy L. Sayers, in her Lord Peter Wimsey mystery novels, has a conversational style of narration, using third person omniscient, hopping from one point-of-view character to another, but it feels seamless because the consistent element is the affectionate treatment of the people in her story. She dips more deeply into the minds of some characters more than others, leaving the latter mysterious or opaque as necessary.

Whether you write in present or past tense, conventional wisdom suggests that you stick to one or the other. It looks like a mistake if you jump back and forth between tenses, unless you do it very well and with purpose. If you find yourself moving from one to the other, decide whether it's deliberate. If it is not, then choose one and be consistent throughout.

You may make a determination early on to use one style, but change your mind partway through. During revision, decide on one and change all other uses to match. Your readers will be grateful.

TONE

When revising your book, consistency is important in many ways. One of the most important is how the story reads. Is your book a tragedy or a comedy? Does it start out sounding playful but descend into despair? Does it begin like a horror story but change halfway through to a farce? The basic tone of your story should be evident from the beginning, so it will attract the right readers, the ones who will enjoy your book the most. Don't try to fool your audience. You might sell the reader one book, but if you disappoint her, you won't sell more.

Begin in your narrative hook, not only setting the reader in time and space, but in mood. Carry the tone throughout the story, changing vocabulary, even sentence length, to match the overall feeling that you wish to produce.

For example, a sweeping epic will have long, lush descriptions, wrapping lovingly around the characters and the environs they inhabit, touching on small details that tell the reader about the life that people lead in that world, and hinting at the wonders and harrowing adventures to come. A hard-boiled detective novel will get to the point. It won't waste the reader's time on fluff. (See what I did there?) Be grand, terse, humorous, dark, grim-dark, squick, playful, encouraging, patient and indulgent, or clinical, depending on the needs of the story itself. The closer you keep your tone consistent, the more likely your reader is to allow that suspension of disbelief you have set up.

That's not to say you can't have tension. Without conflict, you haven't written a story, but a vignette. Rising tension is common to nearly all tales. In a horror novel, that tone will build and build, until your reader refuses to sit with her back to an open door. Relieve that tension occasionally. In *The Keep* by F. Paul Wilson, Nazis and their captives occupy a huge, old castle that is haunted by an intelligent presence that means to pick them off one by one. I won't spoil the brilliant moment, but after building the agonizing suspense for chapters, Wilson relieves the tension in one telling but appropriate scene involving a vampire and a rabbi. The audience will laugh, and breathe again, leaving Wilson to return to setting them on tenterhooks. His tone remains consistent throughout.

Decide how you want the reader to feel while she is reading your book. Match your pacing, vocabulary, and cadence to suit that mood.

THE SCIENCE FICTION OR FANTASY IDEA

If you are writing science fiction or fantasy, the story hinges upon a SF or fantasy concept that will color your plot and affect the world the characters inhabit. This is your suspension of disbelief, that single element that makes your story possible. A genetic mutation makes a character irresistible to those who see him. Cats have psychic abilities. A previous advanced civilization left faster-than-light technology behind on our planet, hidden in a cave. For fantasy, the idea can be as simple as the existence of magic. What permutations and changes that wreaks upon the world are evolutions of that concept. When revising, it is important to make sure you are not throwing in too many unique ideas. Editors call these "kitchen sink" stories for obvious reasons. You get one per story, otherwise you can descend into farce. (On the other hand, if you are writing farce, go for it. That is your suspension of disbelief.)

Have you foreshadowed the possibility of that idea early in the story? As in a mystery, you must be fair to the reader. Don't spring the notion that your teenage protagonist has advanced magical powers at the moment that happens. You can keep the great revelation a secret if you lay small hints that people can perform cantrips, the characters know of enchanted articles that can do great wonders, or that wise women always leave a saucer of milk on the doorstep at night for the fair folk to drink. Show that there have been odd emissions of radiation coming from the ground that can't be put down to the local power plant, or that a startling number of unrelated persons have claimed to been abducted by little gray men, though no one believes them.

Does the climax of the story make use of the idea? If it does not, then you may not have written SF or fantasy, but a story set in a milieu with all the trappings of your preferred genre. If your plot can take place anywhere else, then you might not have written speculative fiction at all. Chances are you started out with a great idea, but it may have fallen by the wayside while you wrote, or you simply never incorporated it into your plot as a necessary element. Go back and see where it fell off your radar.

CONVENTIONS AND TROPES

There are some accepted literary conventions, considered a given shared by everyone, that you may include in your story to make the plot line run more smoothly, such as faster-than-light drive or artificial gravity. Without FTL drive, the trip from Earth to Alpha

Centauri would last four years. Unless the journey is important to your story, you may use that convention to get to the star system and the next part of your plot much faster. Because of readers' familiarity with these concepts in other current books, television shows, and movies, such as *Star Trek*™, they will most likely let the technical handwaving pass without question or lengthy explanation. Conventions can help keep the story going

It's easy to pile on conventions, so watch how many you employ. You don't want your book to be thought of as common, hence boring, space opera. Let your internal editor rein in your impulse to use more than you need.

Tropes are, to quote TVTropes.org, "storytelling shorthand for a concept that the audience will recognize and understand immediately." They're useful for creating a mental picture. If you say "elf," most readers will imagine tall, elegant, magical beings aloof from the concerns of humans. But you don't want to fall into the trap of being accused of copying J.R.R. Tolkien. Describe the ways in which your elves differ (if they do) from the ones in *The Lord of the Rings*, or *Dungeons & Dragons*. Do they have purple skin? Are they cannibals? Set yourself apart from the cliché as soon as you can with good description.

Studying tropes will give you some good ideas, but put your own spin on them.

STORY BIBLE

At this point, you will realize you have a lot of details to keep track of. Continuity is your watchword. You will lose your reader's trust and respect if things change unnecessarily throughout your work. Always look for conflicts and correct them.

One way to manage all this information is with a story bible. All television shows and ongoing movie franchises keep one and issue it to their writers. You should have one, especially if this is part of an ongoing series, or it is the first of what you hope will become a series.

If you have not made a story bible, when you begin to revise is a good time, because you will almost certainly have to refer back to it at least once. There are numerous programs and apps, even websites, that you may use alongside your word processing program (or incorporated in it) to keep track of details, but a notebook or an ordinary Word file is enough. How you organize your facts is up to you, from a simple list to an Excel database or Evernote notebook, but it should be structured so you can find the details you need as quickly as possible. Keep it up to date as you write, and there will be less to do on it when you're ready to revise. All the world-building you have done needs to be recorded. If it's important to your story, it should be noted in your story bible.

Go through your book and make a note of everything below, with the number of the chapter in which it first appears, and the chapter number of any alterations. Peggy appears in chapter one, gets her degree in computer science in chapter five, gets married to Tracy in chapter seventeen. Page numbers are ephemeral, depending on computer pagination. If you move anything, change the entry in your bible. You'll be grateful later for careful record-keeping. Keep it open as a separate file on your computer for easy reference.

The small details are as important as the large ones. Your readers will notice if Peggy has blue eyes in chapter five and green eyes in chapter twenty, and it will diminish their trust in you. So will blowing up the same city five chapters later than you did it the first time.

Every character should have a comprehensive description. Even if some of those details never appear in the novel, you should know them and note them down when you decide upon them. When you begin to write a sequel to your novel, there may be a gap of years or many other books written in between. Chances are very good that you might not remember vital information that made those characters unique. Do yourself a favor and write it all down now while it's fresh.

CHARACTER DESCRIPTIONS AND THEIR RELATIONSHIPS TO ONE ANOTHER

If you never thought about what your character looks like when writing the story, during revisions is the time to create a comprehensive description you can use to flavor the narrative.

Begin with the basics: vital statistics, age, education, likes and dislikes, turn-ons and turn-offs, fears, hopes and dreams, hobbies, talents, and so on. If he has a big family, draw up a family tree. If you're uncertain how to describe his personality, imagine that you are talking about a friend and note the characteristics that make him seem real. This will inform your editing (or writing) process. What is his goal in life? What has stopped him from achieving it so far? The more you know, the more knowledge you can internalize and write *from*.

"Edna, divorced, 56 years old, 5'3", 165 pounds, with most of her weight in her rear end. Silver hair, blue eyes, double chin, little square hands with veins crawling over the backs. She's self-conscious about her wobbly upper arms but proud of her legs. Edna has a graduate degree in chemistry, and manages a department at a pharmaceutical corporation. She is tough on everyone except her son, Sidney, 30, whom she enables by allowing him to live in her basement. She does his laundry, cooks for him every day, and lends him money he never pays back. She won't admit that she loves her job, which she is very good at. She would love to date, but is afraid to take the first step."

Where does she start out, and where does she have to go to succeed? What is her goal in this story? If you didn't use a plotting system, like notecards, sticky notes, or a computer program, you can jot down events, encounters, and important changes in the story bible. What does the character know and not know, by chapter? For example, don't have the character rely upon someone that she hasn't met yet. Or if she has met him, don't have let her not have met him five chapters later. Unless you are writing about time travel, in which case you also need a clearly charted timeline.

TIMELINE

This can be set out as a calendar or a list. If you're not using specific dates, at least number the days in which the events take place. You would be surprised how often a writer discovers an unwanted overlap or gap. A timeline will also help you to discern if an important character, such as the villain, hasn't made a necessary appearance for too long. It might be best to have this one on paper or in a document in which you can draw lines or arrows in between sections (see time travel, above). A timeline can help you with pacing.

If your story takes place during actual historical events, put that into your calendar first, then add the scenes from your book into the squares to parallel those moments. If aliens hitch a ride back to Earth on Apollo 11, that won't happen on July 20th, 1969, the day the Eagle module landed on the Moon, but later, on July 24th.

Anything that will help keep the elements of your story straight and moving forward in a way that works for you is the right way. You can keep a list, or a calendar, or a multi-page diary on which you note all the events as they happen, where it takes place and what characters are involved. For example, bestselling romance author Cherry Adair's *Writers' Bible* (cherryadair.com) explains her method of outlining the story via notecards or sticky notes in a rainbow of colors. Once you have the timeline set out, refer back to it as needed. Remember to revise if you change any of those events, or the discontinuity may create a cascade of bad data all the way to the end of your book.

PLACE NAMES AND DESCRIPTIONS

Former British Prime Minister Winston Churchill once said, "We shape our buildings; thereafter they shape us." The same is true for the locations you have created for your characters. What they inhabit affects the way they act and how they see the world. As editor, you need to make sure the reader will be able to picture the environment where the action takes place. As with characters, describe where you are as soon as you change to a new location. Have you given the reader enough to be able to conjure up a picture from your words? If you have, then no revision is needed, but you may wish to copy those paragraphs into your story bible. The more detailed your saved description, the easier it will be for you to recreate the place for future volumes without having to reread all your earlier books. Consider new readers who come upon your series and binge-read all eighteen volumes in a week; any inconsistencies will be glaring. Save yourself a lot of trouble, and provide the reader a comprehensive image now.

If the locations are fictional, give them as much detail as you can. "N'mlk'at Café, next to the Temple of Logic, serves the best plomeek soup on Vulcan. The café only seats twenty at small tables or the counter that faces the cooking area, but many locals and denizens of the temple socialize outside before or after their meals. Its fame has spread because of its food's quality, not the building's appearance, which is covered with a self-effacing steel blue stucco and a tall, teak-colored wooden door whose edge has become rounded with wear. The savory aromas float in the air for meters outside the building. A stray sehlat mooches around the kitchen door at the rear, waiting for scraps from the cook."

If you are using real-world locations, note your research (i.e., map, magazine article, Wikipedia entry, photo file) for future reference. If you have a good description here, it will save you the work of reconstructing one later on. You can create a Pinterest pinboard, an Evernote folder, or just a photo gallery of real-world places that look like the cities or landscape you describe in your story. Having images to refer to helps a writer to draw better word pictures so your reader can visualize the events of your story.

This is the very essence of world-building, in which you create the world where your story takes place. Geography creates natural boundaries between places, resulting in different cultures growing up fairly close to one another, say on either side of a mountain range or a river. What do the houses look like? Where do people interact? How do they get around? Where do they eat? How do the buildings differ on the rich and poor sides of town? How old is the city? Was it built on the foundations of one that was swept away in a tsunami, or do old structures stand side by side with the newest? Heavy forestation, desert, or the occasional garden?

ITEMS OF IMPORTANCE

Note them by their description, followed by the location of mentions in the manuscript. A pearl necklace with forty five-millimeter pink pearls, given to Peggy by her grandmother, Vanessa Gruce, on her 16th birthday, chapter one. Strand broken in chapter ten, with one pearl lost. A golden ring (chapter twelve), plain except when thrown into a fire, when fiery red letters in ancient elvish spell out a sinister poem (chapter fifteen). A sword with an inscription reading "Whoso pulleth this sword out of this stone and anvil will be rightwise crowned king of England," appears in the prologue. The characters encounter it in chapter eight. Jot down as much detail as you can when you envision an item. Your reader will want to know everything there is to know.

THE SCIENCE OF MAGIC

One of the most important functions of both a revision and your bible is to make sure the unusual elements in your story work. At this, a good bible excels. If fantasy, you will likely be using magic, so you need to know how it works in your world. Your magic system can be anything from "everyone can do any spell," to "you must have the nose hair of a virgin elephant, a square inch of red silk, ten thousand gold pieces and five years magical training to perform this cantrip." The more complex it is, the more comprehensive your notes on it should be. Magic has physics as much as science does: unless yours is of the "everyone can do everything" variety, there will be costs and scarcity to using a spell. Keep track of those. It can add rising tension to your story if your character is down to his last dragon scale and facing a fire troll.

If you're borrowing the system from a different source (such as *Dungeons & Dragons*), note specific references (divination, page 32, *Player's Guide*). If you have created an original, this section might grow up to be a small grimoire, with spells or magical rites delineated in detail. Even if you never explain how a ritual is performed, you need to know all of this yourself. Please, for heaven's sake and potential cries of outrage from your readers, do not use D&D as an obvious source. Inspiration only. The rest should come from your imagination.

THE MAGIC OF SCIENCE

If you're writing science fiction, make a note of scientific principles vital to the story, unless you are a scientist who has this information at your fingertips. Then, refer to these notes whenever revising parts of your story that include them. This can include URLs or hyperlinks to web pages where you found information that you used, book titles and page numbers of important facts, letters or e-mails between you and a scientist you asked for information. Having a bibliography is useful if a fan wants to know more, or if you need to defend one of your facts to your editor.

Keep in mind that what you have written is *fiction*. If you need something to happen that is impossible, just make it plausible and consistent throughout your story. See *Hollyweird Science* by Kevin R. Grazier and Steven Cass (Springer, 2015). A note from my first editor, the late Brian Thomsen: no more than ten percent of the hard-won research that you did to write a fiction book should ever appear in it. Don't air your education. You are there to entertain your reader. While you might be interested in every little detail of molecular biology, anything that doesn't move the story along does not belong in it. This goes for anything else you have studied in order to write your book.

SOCIAL STANDINGS AND CUSTOMS

All stories are about people (or sentient beings), and those beings have a culture of some sort. Consistency in presenting that culture is vital. Once you have established how people interact, the reader will expect that as the norm in your story or series. Where it deviates must be explained in some fashion, or changed. Barbara the Barbarian refuses to pray before meals as everyone else does. If you had her do that on purpose, show that she is protesting against the custom for her own reasons, or was never taught how to revere the local deities. If you omitted her joining in the prayer, correct that now.

Good notes can assist you in revising or cutting jarring scenes that confuse or annoy your readers. How do the characters address one another, or those of different stations? Who goes by what title (if any)? How do they greet and say farewell to one another? What is the order of precedence when a procession enters the king's court? Are visitors and strangers welcome? Do they receive glares or are instantly seen as potential mugging victims? What is the fate of criminals?

What rituals exist in your world? Frequently, a writer will start out with some very cool and interesting practices, and forget all about them by the end of a book. Read your notes and incorporate them if they have fallen by the wayside.

GOVERNMENT

Someone is running things, be it a senate, a church, a computer, the old lady who lives on the edge of the village with thirty cats, or a combination of all of these. Even if the government does not appear directly in your story, the structure of control will be evident throughout. Again, once you know how things are set up, it will inform your writing. If they never appear, you don't have to name the king, the power broker, or the five most important cats, just be aware of what influence they wield throughout their realm. How do those people ascend to a position of authority? Is it by inheritance, election, or force of arms? Even good rulers can create onerous and heavy regulations that interfere with the character's life.

Does your character need to get permission to study magic or open a shop? What duty does s/he owe to the government? Does she have to do obligatory military service, or can she be ordered to serve the queen as a handmaiden? If your character must bribe five different levels of officials, from a minister down to the village guardsman, that adds color to the narrative, as well as adding tension to the story itself. And what duty and protection does the government owe to your character and her family? Who mediates disputes and passes judgements? Who raises an army or sets up the defense shield for a colony? Does the government provide grants or other assistance? Who runs the space program? Where is confidential data kept, and who has keys to the database? Who sets the value of currency and creates legal coinage or other forms of symbolic exchange, and what is that value? Does it vary from kingdom to kingdom or planet to planet?

Is the system of government too top heavy for the economy? Most of them are. That can add to the conflict, or the humor of a situation, when the character discovers that he can play one department against another.

Knowledge of how the government runs will add a layer of reality to a story that may be thin on factual structure. While stories about teenagers getting hold of a spaceship are common in middle-school literature, such things won't fly (literally) in a novel for adults. Know how the system works. If you didn't pay attention in civics class, this topic might be a stretch to study, but it's worth it to see how power flows.

ECONOMY

Where does food come from, and where does waste go in your world? Is there a massive international conglomerate that owns all the farms or hydroponic systems shipped directly to consumers, or is the source of edibles a host of smallholdings who hawk their goods in the market once a week? Are avocados as plentiful as mosquitoes in one city and as rare as gold in the next?

Do people pay one another with goods or with symbolic currency (see above), or both? Most pre-industrial nations used some form of barter economy, trading like value for like directly. If you pay your doctor with a dozen eggs or a bag of wheat, that's bartering. If you pay her with a coin that represents the value of a dozen eggs, that's symbolic currency. Dollars, pounds sterling, yuan, and euros are stored value, as is a letter of credit, a check, credit cards, or an IOU. What do your characters use in the marketplace, the inn, or the fuel depot on a space station? What's in your character's pocket? How do they dispose of waste? How do they pay for oxygen, or cattle, or housing, boots, and clothing? What's the source of all these things, and how much value is lost or added by middlemen? The tailor makes goods from the cloth provided to her by the weaver, who got the rovings from the shearer, who took the fleece off the sheep cared for by the shepherd, who works for the squire who owns both flock and grazing land. Many other people had their hands on the goods your character buys. Does your character interact with them, or is aware of them?

Innumerable beloved sagas have nonfunctional economic systems, such as Anne McCaffrey's Dragonriders series. Of notable exception are works by L.E. Modesitt, who is an economist as well as a great epic fantasy writer, and has lovingly crafted working economic models. Read one of his novels for an example. If you are plausible in your world-building, the minutiae of how goods come and go and how money works are not necessarily important, but make notes of where it is and keep that consistent. This section is irrevocably tied to that of government, but the smaller interchanges keep the world running as much as the major ones do.

Here's one of the places where you can so easily fall down the rabbit hole of research. Be as economical with your investigations as you are with applying that research to your writing. You want to finish your story and turn it in so you can go on to the next one. Learn only what you need to, and save the interesting books, links, and URLs for later.

RELIGION AND MYTHOLOGY

When you're revising, make sure to look not only at what your characters believe, but at the institutions that support those beliefs. Not every story has or needs a comprehensive church system operating within it, but nearly every culture will have a common world-building mythology that informs it, and sometimes both. Rome is reputed to have been founded by Romulus and Remus, orphaned twin brothers who had been rescued from a storm at sea, then suckled by Luperca, a female wolf. It has since become the world seat for an entirely unrelated major religion. Your world could have such depth in its origins. The opportunity is yours to exploit. What customs have grown up around the core beliefs? Are there specific garments the initiates wear? What rituals do they practice, and what objects do they require? People give their best work to their religions, such as great cathedrals, master-level artwork, and musical compositions in tribute to their gods. If you're inspired to write hymns or chants, that would add interesting color to your work. (And if there is no good place to put them, keep them in your notes instead.) Does one gender or race hold primacy? If so, how do they treat those who are not members of the elite?

Religions have adherents, both the ordinary faithful as well as many tiers of priesthood or responsibility for overseeing the rules and strictures. Make notes of which characters belong to the religion or religions, where they fit in the hierarchy, and to whom they answer. What holidays do they have? Support for religieuses and the buildings or land they occupy comes from somewhere. Does your character have to tithe earnings or serve in one of these locations part of the year (or is it their job)? Does that support create hardship for the ordinary person?

Again, much of this might never appear in the book, but if it matters to the story line, you ought to know it and keep track of details.

ALTERATIONS AND AMENDMENTS

If there are changes to anything in your bible, they ought to be a function of the story, not a lapse in memory. Your story bible is akin to your conscience. You should be aware of its influence while you work.

REVISE AS NECESSARY

The beginning of your book will feel awkward once you go back to read it again, because your understanding of the story has matured while you were writing the rest of it. Once you have written several thousand words, you will usually find yourself falling into a voice that will carry you through the rest of the manuscript, particularly if you are able to have written it in a contiguous period. Because life happens, you may have been forced to start and stop, perhaps again and again for days, weeks, or years. What it will mean for your revision is that you may have changed the way you narrate the story, perhaps several times. Smooth out the narrative voice so that it is consistent from the beginning to the end. Your reader may not be aware of what you have done, but they will feel comfortable with the continuity.

Once you have completed your first draft, you will almost certainly need to rewrite the beginning, because it is attached to a book that isn't the same one you began. That's normal. Everybody feels around for style until they get moving. Don't make the mistake of leaving the opening awkward and unpolished compared with the rest of the manuscript. Take the knowledge you now have, reread the ending, and go back to the start. The first pages are what will draw the reader in (see Narrative Hook). They are your sales pitch. It needs to fit with what now comes afterward.

Caution: do not incorporate events or revelations into that beginning that come later. Refer to your timeline if necessary. You're just cleaning up the foyer so your reader will be comfortable walking into your living room.

If you have trouble imagining how the reader will experience the narration (and the dialogue; more on that later), either read the text aloud to yourself, have someone else read it to you, or have a device read it. The last will lack mood and inflection, but removing distractions might help you to hear the character of your prose better. Some writers read their text backward to catch errors and repetition. Until how you wrote the book is no longer uppermost in your mind, you will almost certainly roll past some mistakes, as they will seem perfectly normal to you.

With your plot firmly in mind, go through the manuscript with a critical eye. Are your characters behaving in logical and natural ways as they encounter the obstacles that you have put in their way? Do they approach those obstacles as reasonable people would? (No, babysitter in the horror movie! Don't go down into the basement to investigate the creepy noise!) Don't have your characters do stupid things just to advance your plot. The reader will stop dead at logical inconsistencies and may put the book down for good. Unless there is a very good reason, people will not willingly plunge into danger. Make them do it.

What makes your character leave her daily life and go off on the quest you set her? If you did not include that initiating incident, but evidence exists in your story that there was one, draw a picture for your reader. Did your hobbit suddenly realize that the heirloom ring that his uncle left for him attracts Ringwraiths?

How's your rising tension? Do you worry about the protagonist making it through her journey as she goes? When Lessa impressed the sole remaining queen dragon on Pern, as in Anne McCaffrey's *Dragonflight*, keeping Ramoth alive and well was only one of the problems she faced. The growing evidence that the ancient scourge of Thread was approaching made her consider drastic action to save her world, even risking her life and that of the one breeding dragon left. Make the stakes high enough that your reader is sitting on the edge of his seat. Occasional releases, such as humorous interludes in a horror story, help the reader to cope with the strain of unremitting fear or dread. Tension should continue to rise until the crisis point of the story, when the protagonist must cope with the worst possible event of her life.

If you build the suspense higher and higher, did you build in relief valves, what Blake Snyder calls "Fun and Games," so the reader can relax a little? Despite the growing seriousness of the situation, Lessa gets to fly that dragon into the skies over her homeworld. How awesome is that?

Don't shy away from the hard scenes. The reader needs to know that the stakes are high. If you feel as though the scene is boring, consider whether it needs to be there at all. If so, rewrite it so it fulfills the purpose it had when you wrote it in the first place. Don't suggest that a necessary and meaningful scene existed, but you couldn't be bothered to write it. Write it. The reader needs to experience it and understand it.

What did the protagonist need to accomplish? Blake Snyder says that what the main character starts out to achieve often changes midway through the story to what he *needs* to do. Did your character undergo that transformation?

Do you build to a satisfying conclusion? You have promised the reader a spectacular payoff. Make it worth her while for reading all the way through your book. Novels provide escape and wish fulfillment. We're entertainers. Give the reader what she is hoping for.

DESCRIPTION

While I touched on this in the Narrative Hook section, it continues to be vital throughout your work. Thoughtful description shows that you are thinking on the reader's behalf. You can see in your own mind what your world looks like. Until you put that on the page, the reader cannot share your vision. Long stretches of dialogue with no description are tedious. Long stretches of unattributed dialogue are confusing and annoying.

Show, don't tell is something writers hear all the time from teachers and pundits. The more dynamic elements you add to a statement about a character's action, the better your story will read. "He was shocked at her outburst," is dull. "His eyes widened at her furious response," is much more interesting and only one word longer.

The reader wants emotional and physical reactions and interactions from your characters. They won't come across as real people if they are merely spouting words at one another.

Not only visual images should be added, but other sensory input. How does your world smell? What sounds are going on in the background? Is music playing? What physical sensations is your character experiencing? Draw as vivid a picture as you can. If you have not included these elements while you are writing the story, add them in revision, three or more to a page.

Don't let the description get in the way of the action. Incorporate it into the character's observations of his surroundings. Show the reader the small details that make your world memorable.

PACING AND CADENCE

Look at how the whole story reads as you go through it. A novel will fall into a kind of rhythm. Your chapters don't need to be all the same length, but their structure should be consistent. Get into the scene as late as you can before the action begins, and get out as soon as possible when it ends. A chapter can comprise a single scene, or a few short but related scenes, such as the heroine escaping from a trap, then the villain responding to hearing his plan to capture her failed.

Your style will dictate how long your chapters run. Just as jokes are funnier when they are brief and to the point, humorous novels tend to have shorter chapters, one to three thousand words. Mainstream fiction also often has short chapters, as well as a punchier, more spare style with less description than genre fiction. Dramatic novels need more room to build up and tell the tale. As you finish revising each chapter, ask yourself if that last one was too long or too short. Did it jump around or drag?

You should almost sense a beat as you begin and end each chapter. If there's a gap or a false note, investigate whether you have two chapters that ought to be one, or an overlong chapter that should be broken into two or more.

In this stage, you should be paring away narration that bogs down the story. Does an element you have included move the plot? Does it tell you something vital about a character? No? Then it needs to come out. Save it for your own files, or the *Guide to Your World* that you publish someday. It wouldn't be unusual for the story bible to be nearly as long as the first novel.

End each chapter, if you can, on a cliffhanger, an element that compels your reader to want to turn the page, no matter how long after midnight they are reading. Dan Brown, in his Da Vinci Code books, never fails to drag the reader irresistibly from one chapter into the next. Study his writing and consider what elements you can steal, er, employ yourself.

You should have been studying your chosen market to see what readers expect from your type of book.

Cadence also suggests the rhythm of the words themselves. If you are telling the story of a South Sea islander, the words might come in a calypso beat. War stories have a more terse, guttural, harsh diction. The pattern you use is another tool to envelop the reader in a cocoon of your storytelling and make them feel as though they are in your world. If you don't get the sense of being there, examine that now. Find the rough edges and file them down by adding a relaxing beat here and there, or sharpen your reader's attention by thrusting barked orders and abrupt responses at them.

ACTION SCENES

Remember the part about ruthlessly cutting unneeded words that slow the story? When you are revising action scenes, this becomes more likely. Your reader should be just as focused on action as your characters. Therefore, do not distract her from what is going on. Action concentrates attention on a very small area. If your character is in a fight with someone, his attention is on his opponent's eyes and hands, or their ship in the viewscreen. Extraneous material only serves to interrupt

—unless your intention is to break that concentration. Focus only opens outward as other elements to which the character must pay attention join the scene. If someone is coming at your character with a machete, he should be thinking in the here and now. Going off on a narrative tangent about how he offered his first sword at the altar of his god at age fifteen and had a party thrown in his honor would in the real world get him killed for inattention. Treat action scenes as if you are in them.

To help raise the sense of immediacy, shorten your sentences in those scenes to short, declarative phrases. They will make your reader breathe faster, and add to the sense of excitement. (It's a trick, but it works.)

"The Silver Turtle unsheathed his sword and lunged forward. Just in time, Bob dodged to the right. The gleaming point missed his ribs by inches. Bob fumbled for his war hammer. It slipped out of his fingers and hit the steel floor with a *clang*. The Silver Turtle grinned and lunged again."

Don't build long, elaborate sentences that can get the reader tangled up. Save internal musings for when the Silver Turtle is tied up and waiting for the City Guard.

APPROPRIATE VOCABULARY

As I have mentioned before, word choices are very important. Your story will feel age-inappropriate to small children if you use fifteen-syllable words or to adults if you use nothing but short, choppy declarative sentences. By now you have identified your tone and voice. Lists are available of words used in books for children, middle-schoolers, and young adults. Never talk down to your reader. Assume they *can* look up a difficult word, but it's wise not to make them have to put down the book to do it. Explain unusual vocabulary in context.

"Nina gawked as Ivan stepped out of the regenerator, looking fifty years younger in a matter of minutes."

Don't fall into the trap of using an elaborate word unless you really know what it means. The humorous character Mrs. Malaprop, from the 1775 play "The Rivals" by Richard Sheridan, became a noun, "malapropism," for her use of wrong but similarly sounding words. If you like the sound of a word, but it's not one you normally use, look it up and make sure it's the one you want.

Whether you use cursing is also guided by the age group for whom you are writing. Comedian George Carlin's "Seven Words You Can Never Say on Television" is a good guideline for avoiding pitfalls. Kids will have heard them on the schoolground anyhow, but don't limit your sales by filling your books with profanity.

Swearing is common in numerous walks of life and places like locker rooms, so those words will be appropriate coming from characters in those venues. Selina Rosen's humorous novel *Queen of Denial* is so laden with cursing that it turns off some readers, but is amusing to the audience she is trying to draw.

Otherwise, cursing should be used for emphasis. Maledictions and invective will draw attention every time they appear. You're already putting everything in your manuscript on purpose. Swear words are no different than verbs or adjectives. Know your market, and use vocabulary accordingly.

GRAMMAR

Use proper grammar in your narration. As mentioned above, most of the time you will want your narration to disappear from the reader's attention to let the story shine. Don't leave your reader baffled by what you are trying to say. If you're not a good judge of your own writing, ask someone else to look at it.

Vary your sentence structure. Make friends with your dynamic verbs. Using forms of the verb "to be" over and over again gets tedious in no time, and sets your reader at a remove from the action. Break yourself of the "was" habit. "It was a dark and stormy night," the well-known and much parodied phrase from Edward Bulwer-Lytton's 1830 novel *Paul Clifford*, goes on to describe that dark and stormy night, but he could easily have begun with the second phrase instead:

"It was a dark and stormy night; the rain fell in torrents—except at occasional intervals, when it was checked by a violent gust of wind which swept up the streets (for it is in London that our scene lies), rattling along the housetops, and fiercely agitating the scanty flame of the lamps that struggled against the darkness."

Isn't that more effective?

Repetition of words ought to be used for emphasis, not because you can't be bothered to use synonyms. Conventional wisdom suggests that you count fifty words before making use of a unique word or phrase again. If there is no other word, say, because the object or verb is one you created for the story, there are still terms like thing, item, piece, element, and so on, to take its place.

Limit the use of sentence fragments. Too often, they're subordinate phrases that have been unfairly cut loose from the sentence before or after them. Reunite the poor things with their parent phrases. The style is good for emphasis, but annoying in overuse.

When you have more than one character of the same gender in a scene, be careful not to confuse the reader with too many he's and she's. "He threw a punch, but had to duck when he swung a chain at his head." A remedy for this problem is to name the characters or use distinctive physical traits instead of the third person pronoun.

PUNCTUATION AND SPELLING

You're in charge of making your book as readable as possible. Spelling and punctuation count.

If you're not a good speller, spellcheck is your friend, but not your best friend. It can't detect whether you're using a homonym. If you use "right" when you meant "rite," "your" when you needed "you're," or "discrete" when "discreet" was what you intended, it won't flag the errors. Go back to see what the word processing program has underlined, but bear in mind that in every science fiction or fantasy novel, there are almost certain to be made-up words or names that Word will declare are wrong. If you're using a program that allows you to add to the stored vocabulary, add your names and other terms. That will make it easier to scan the rest of the file.

Improper use or a lack of punctuation is distracting. Most common is the dearth of commas between interjections or names in the following sentences. "Wow can I have one?" should have a comma after Wow. "Martha your the best," was just autocorrected by Word. I had to change it back to show the mistakes of a missing comma and an incorrect homonym.

If you're just not good at punctuation and grammar, many books are available to help, such as William Strunk and E.B. White's[1] *Elements of Style*, or the *Chicago Manual of Style*. Most editors use one or both of these.

MAKING YOUR BOOK OBSOLETE

What is common knowledge here and now in your own milieu is not necessarily widely known in the rest of the world. While you can write in a *Star Trek*™ novel, "Mr. Spock beamed back to the *Enterprise* after eating a bowl of plomeek soup prepared for him by Amanda," you shouldn't depend on future audiences knowing any of those terms or relationships. Nothing dates a story faster than pop culture references or current slang. You don't know what will survive the ages. Don't write that book that has to be footnoted to be understood.

INFODUMPS

You may find that you have several extended gouts of information that you desperately want the reader to know. Now is the time to break them up. What well-respected science fiction author C.J. Cherryh refers to as "cold, indigestible lumps of exposition" are deadly to the pacing of any scene, but most especially to action. They also take the reader out of the moment. Have you gone on for several pages with a flashback or an explanation of something? However important that information is, the journey of the main character(s) is more important. Can you find a way to continue to show the scene while enlightening the reader as to the history or facts you need them to know as a function of that scene? Work it into other observations, or have the characters refer to the parts that are necessary for the book to function.

DIALOGUE

Mort Walker, the original cartoonist of "Beetle Bailey," said you should be able to distinguish each character by its silhouette alone. Using the same wisdom, your reader should be able to tell the difference between characters by the way they speak. If everyone sounds like you, or phrases their sentences precisely the same, you have the opportunity to change that now. Your knowledge of your characters, their background, age, education, experiences, and all of the facets that make them interesting will have a bearing on the way they talk. Have you taken advantage of all of those? Spock would say, "Indeed." Buffy would say, "Whatever." Making their diction unique will help do away with the confusion created by unattributed dialogue, where you have streams of speech without mentioning, "he said," "she said," "Spock said," "Buffy replied."

As above with the narration, if you read your dialogue aloud to yourself or have someone else read it, you can see what phrases roll trippingly off the tongue or make you run out of breath. Your readers will read your book aloud in their minds. If you can't finish a sentence without gasping in more air, find a place to break it. People do not usually emit long spates of dialogue without breaks. They stop and breathe. So should your characters.

Dialogue is not conversation; conversation is not dialogue. If you were to transcribe a conversation you had in real life onto a page, most readers would wait impatiently for the exchange to get to the point. Real conversations are boring except to those who are involved in them.

Dialogue should help to move the story along in the same way that description and exposition do. Unless your character has a reason for mindlessly blathering along, cut their speeches down to what needs to be there. Don't waste the reader's time.

SAID WORDS

Said," like proper grammar, is virtually invisible to the reader. Harlan Ellison, master stylist, took one of my co-authors to task on his overuse of alternatives. With that in mind, feel free to use other words occasionally if "said" is too weak. "Shouted," "snarled," "murmured," "replied," "retorted," and so on, are useful for creating mood. Treat them like salt; a few add flavor. Too many render the results unpalatable.

The sentences using any "said" word are structured with a comma between the dialogue and the speaker, i.e., "I'm just glad to be here," Martha said.

If you choose to have the speaker take any other action that is not a synonym for "said," then the sentence ends with a final punctuation mark in between the dialogue and speaker. "I can't believe you bought me the ring." Olivia clasped her hands. "I love it!"

WHOOPS, I FORGOT TO ...

Be making a list of things you forgot to put into the book on a side list, and insert them when you come to the right place. Above all, go back and foreshadow when appropriate in earlier chapters. It will pull the reader right out of the story if suddenly when faced with a ten-foot troll your character remembers that he's a sixteenth dan black belt, when you have never mentioned it before. As in alternate history, one little change can completely alter the path of your story. If you introduced a show-stopper of a change late in the book, consider whether you have hinted about it enough earlier, or if this is something that negates everything you wrote before. If you really like the way the story was going, leave out the earthshaking revelations. If they're vital to the conclusion, you'll have to do some rewriting.

MORE RESEARCH

If you need it, do it now. It may change your story line substantially. Know when to ignore non-relevant facts in favor of your narrative. (See Science, above) If you can make departures from reality plausible, your reader will go on that ride with you. By this stage, you'll know if you have created a reasonable reality. Don't fall down the rabbit hole of Wikipedia or other sources. Set yourself a deadline and stick to it.

THOSE LITTLE DETAILS

Writers become temporary experts on subjects when writing a book that involves them. Now is the time to see if you can sprinkle in any more of those little details that insiders will know means you really know what you're talking about. It's also the time to remove the ones that are inaccurate and will jar the reader with their wrongness. Anyone who is unfamiliar with the layout of the city of Chicago is unlikely to know that the route taken by the Blues Brothers on the car chase through their eponymous 1980 movie is impossible. (That made it all the funnier for those of us who live here.)

WORD COUNT

In a short story, this is a vital consideration. Editors are only so flexible when it comes to accepting a piece below the bottom or above the top of their word count. Here's where all the suggestions above will help you to refine what can stay and what must go. Stories start when something changes. Barring a little flavor to set the reader in time and space, you want to begin with a bang that drags your reader into your world.

Does it end with a whimper or a hurrah? Have you finished the arc of energy, and you're now just dribbling words because you don't know when to stop? Read it over to see where the story really ends, and either move what comes afterward into the body of the story or cut it. Your flow will be all the better for the edit.

Many book publishers also have a word limit, frequently around ninety thousand words. They have good financial reasons for keeping to that, but most especially that every additional folio of eight pages costs money. Widening the spine of the book costs money. Shipping fewer books in a box costs money. They economize by controlling the size of the book itself, and that devolves down to you, the author. If your book is going to be substantially larger than most of what is published by your house, consider your alternatives:

—You can cut it down to size.

—You can, with the editor's (and marketing department's) permission, split it into two or more volumes. (The same goes for magazines, if your particular periodical ever serializes stories.) That will require finding natural stopping places that complete one part of the story arc in a satisfying manner but leaving it obvious that the greater plot line will continue, and writing new beginnings for the second (and third, etc.) section without dumping massive quantities of exposition on the reader.

—You can withdraw it and send it elsewhere.

—You can publish it yourself.

During the revision process is the most likely time you need to have this discussion with your editor. If you have a publisher, alternatives three and four are by far the least desirable, as it detracts from the relationship you have established with them.

Do your best to make it work within the guidelines that have been given to you. Few books, from the humblest chapbooks to the biggest bestsellers, have ever been written that wouldn't have benefitted from a little (or a lot of) judicious editing. If that means going over it carefully, sentence by sentence and phrase by phrase, to see what can be deleted, you'll make it a better book and learn more about your craft along the way.

FLESHING IT OUT

Publishing houses also exist that love a good long saga, where one hundred fifty thousand words is not considered too long. Don't overindulge in wordspasms, but take the opportunity to grow your world around your plot. You may also have learned more about your characters as you have continued to write. Examine where you can put in additional insights that make the characters more well-rounded and will help the reader understand their motivation. The side plot lines that tie up at the end will also benefit from additional scrutiny. However, do not use up the extra word count just because you have it. If your reader doesn't need what you plan to say, leave it out. Better a compelling, concise read than a sprawling and incomprehensible epic. Excess verbiage sucks all the energy out of a scene.

NOT WORKING IT TO DEATH

It's completely possible to overwork a story. If it begins to feel stale to you when you've gone over it several times, step away from it, just as you did in the beginning. Keep the story as fresh as you can, while solving the problems that you saw when you began the edit. If you're bored by your book, the reader will be, too. Remember what you loved about the book when you began to write it.

If you need to go back to a previous draft and rescue things you cut out because they were vital color, do it.

You want to compel readers to stay with you through the entire story and be happy they read the ending. Give yourself breaks.

FINAL THOUGHTS

Your protagonist must evolve in some way, either by succeeding and learning something, or failing and learning something. Did she grow? Does the reader understand how she changed? If you brought the story to this point but forgot to state how the protagonist resolved her situation, do it now.

I know you're tired. This is a lot of work. Revising is not as much fun as writing the book, but it's a necessary step to make it publishable.

But you did it! Congratulations!

---

1. Yes, that E.B. White, who wrote *Charlotte's Web*.

FURTHER CONSIDERATIONS

OTHER PEOPLE'S COPYRIGHTS

Have you quoted from a song, poem, book, or movie that came out in the US after 1923? Then that work may still be under copyright, if not to the original author, then to her or his heirs. Check the copyright date! If you absolutely must use that quote, and you have not already obtained permission, do it now, not after you have submitted the story or book to your publisher or uploaded it to an online service. Many copyright holders will allow a single-use of their material. Others will ask for a fee. Find that out now, because your contract with any publisher or online service requires that you have created an original work that includes nothing that will cause anyone or any entity to sue the publisher. You will incur all appropriate legal fees in a lawsuit. "Fair use" does not apply to a work of fiction.

TRADEMARKS

The same goes for trademarks. You may have noticed in some books and stories a well-known name may be accompanied by the tiny letters ™ in superscript after the words. That acknowledges the phrase is trademarked. Such words as Kleenex™, Xerox™, *Star Trek*™, even Mickey Mouse™ are trademarks of their respective corporations. If you need to include that designation, this is your opportunity. You can't use trademarked characters in your work without written permission (although mentions are allowed), and unless you are writing official tie-in fiction or subsidiary work (like computer games), the chances are poor that you will get it. Respect copyrights and trademarks as you hope others will respect your created words and names.

(This is not the same as using a quote in reviews. As a reviewer, you're not making a profit from the use of copyrighted material; quite the opposite. You are trying to help the copyright holder make money.)

If you require more precise information, attorney Richard Stim has published a book called *Getting Permission* (Oct 2016) and has overview data at this URL: https://fairuse.stanford.edu/overview/faqs/copyright-basics/ It's costly, but cheaper than a lawsuit.

FORMATTING

Every publisher has guidelines on its website or social media page. You may e-mail or ship your book directly, or be directed to use a submission bot or aggregator. Unlike the pirate code, these are not mere guidelines but imperatives. Obey the publisher. You want them to buy your book.

Most of the time, editors expect manuscripts in a common format of one side of standard bond paper, either 8 1/2" x 11" or A4 size, white, double-spaced, serif typeface like Courier or Times New Roman, 12-point type. Do not get goofy and use a distinctive typeface to stand out. Your story should set you apart from the masses, not your formatting.

There is a setting on most word processing programs that prevents a second double spacing from appearing in between paragraphs of the same type. Check it. That additional space prevents easy comprehension of your manuscript and wastes paper or room.

You must put a header on the top of every page with your title, your name, and the page number to avoid confusion if the manuscript falls on the floor. On the first page of a short story manuscript, put your contact information, and your word count in the upper right-hand corner. Space down to line 13, and center your title. Below that goes your name. Space down, indent, and begin your first paragraph. For a book, create a cover page with the title and your name centered. Contact information can go in the upper right or bottom left corner with the word count. You do not need to add a copyright notice. Under current law, your work is copyrighted to you as soon as you write it. Formal registration can wait until you sell the book.

All your paragraphs should be indented, not left-justified. Begin each chapter after a page break.

Current style dictates only one space after a final punctuation mark, not two, as those of us who learned to type a long time ago were taught. If you can't break the old habit, use universal search and replace to take out the second space. Italicize internal thoughts, dream sequences, flashbacks (to a certain extent), and possibly telepathic communications (your style for this latter may vary). Emphasized words should also be italicized, as are ship names, book titles, and other designations. Rarely will all-caps or underlining appear in books.

OUTSIDE HELP

EDITORS

If you are self-publishing, as many writers are these days, I recommend hiring an editor, if for no other reason than you will never spot all of your own typographical errors. A good editor will be worth the money. Budget for it. Ask for recommendations from fellow self-pubbed friends, or from another author whose work has that professional sparkle you crave. If you have an agent who edits his clients' work, put it into his hands.

This editor will take the place of the pre-publication staff at a traditional or even a small press publisher. You can hire one to do any or all of the following:

Copy-editing. Going through the manuscript and checking for grammatical and spelling errors. Spellcheck will not tell you whether you have used the wrong homonym. An editor will.

Continuity errors. If you didn't see that Peggy's eye color has changed, the editor will.

Story or developmental editing. This is a conversation, and will cost you more than a simple copy-editor's fee, but will more than pay for itself in improved readership and reviews. Did you achieve what you set out to write? If you tried to make a bad decision work, but it really doesn't, and you can't see the way out of the corner into which you painted yourself, a hired professional can give you advice on what to do to fix it. She or he will not rewrite it for you. You're the author. You will make the decision and the changes according to your lights. In the end, it's your name on the cover, but keep in mind that a pro will have read hundreds if not thousands of other manuscripts and helped them go on to be successful releases. You're paying for their expertise. Consider well what they tell you.

BETA READERS

Not every author uses them, but it's good to have at least one person who will tell you the truth about your book, hopefully with tact. Members of writing groups have a group who will read or listen to an excerpt and will give their reactions.

As with a professional editor, it's still your story in the end. You have every right not to take their suggestions. A friend might have fallen in love with a character that you know you have to kill in a few chapters. They might hate dystopia, horror, or romance, and dislike your story on principle. Their prejudices are not your problem, but you must be aware of them.

Ask them if the world seems plausible to them. What does and doesn't work for them, and why? Unlike a professional, though, you must be careful not to overwork your volunteer readers. Keep your questions short and to the point, asking only those things that you really cannot decide on your own.

You must be a good judge of whether any commenter is being brutally honest or simply brutal. If you find a person who is a good natural editor, treat them well. You'll need them again.

EXPERTS

They're helpful when you're reaching outside your own sphere of experience. If you're writing about a profession in which you have never worked, hand those scenes to a friendly plumber, chiropractor, astrophysicist, opera singer, and ask them to point out errors. You'll get more of those little details (see above) that will stimulate your imagination further and make a scene come to life. Asking an expert is far faster than having to learn a lifetime of a skill or twenty years' education.

You may need to pay for their time. That might only be a beer or a meal, or it could be a fee per hour (get that detail hammered out before you start asking questions). Consider it part of the cost of doing business. Even if you publish through a traditional or small press, this expense is one you must incur yourself, but it might be worth it. On the other hand, experts are so seldom asked to explain how they know what they know, instead of just being asked to do their job, they might answer your questions with no strings attached (except that you will, of course, mention them in the acknowledgements of your book).

Above all, get your manuscript in shape so that all the editor has to do is read it, fight for it in the marketing meeting, and send you a contract. Naturally, while all this is going on, you've written your next book, and are revising that, too.

Happy rewriting!

ABOUT THE AUTHOR

A native Chicagoan, Jody Lynn Nye is a *New York Times* bestselling author of more than fifty books and 165 short stories. As a part of Bill Fawcett & Associates (she is the "& Associates"), she has helped to edit more than two hundred books, including forty anthologies, with a few under her own name. She and Bill are the authors of *Conventional Wisdom*, another in the Million Dollar Writing series for WordFire Press.

Her solo work tends toward the humorous side of SF and fantasy. Along with her individual writing, Jody has collaborated with several notable professionals in the field, including Anne McCaffrey, Robert Asprin, John Ringo, and Piers Anthony. She collaborated with Robert Asprin on a number of books in his famous Myth-Adventures series, and has continued both that and his Dragons Wild series since his death in 2008. Jody runs the two-day intensive writers' workshop at DragonCon, every Labor Day weekend in Atlanta, GA. She is also a judge for the Writers of the Future contest, the largest speculative fiction contest in the world.

Jody lives in the northwest suburbs of Chicago, with her husband Bill Fawcett, a writer, game designer, military historian, and book packager, and three feline overlords, Athena, Minx, and Marmalade. Check out her websites at https://jodynye.net/ and mythadventures.net. She is on Facebook as Jody Lynn Nye and Twitter @JodyLynnNye.

IF YOU LIKED ... ONCE MORE, WITH FEELING, YOU MIGHT ALSO ENJOY:

Pros & Cons
by Jody Lynn Nye & Bill Fawcett

On Being a Dictator
by Kevin J. Anderson & Martin L. Shoemaker

Writing as a Team Sport
by Kevin J. Anderson & Rebecca Moesta

OTHER WORDFIRE PRESS TITLES BY
JODY LYNN NYE

Mythology 101
Mythology Abroad
Advanced Mythology
Higher Mythology

A Circle of Celebrations
Launch Pad
The Magic Touch
Pros & Cons
Strong Arm Tactics

Taylor's Ark
Medicine Show
The Lady and the Tiger

Our list of other WordFire Press authors and titles is always growing. To find out more and to see our selection of titles, visit us at:

WordFirepress.com

www.ingramcontent.com/pod-product-compliance
Lightning Source LLC
Chambersburg PA
CBHW071221070526
44584CB00019B/3107

9781680570656